Dedication

Margaret Mitchell at portable typewriter that launched a legend

Courtesy Atlanta Journal-Constitution Sunday Magazine

MARGARET MITCHELL'S imagination peopled *Gone With the Wind* with legendary characters. They were crafted from the material of history and animated with the substance of life. Though a reticent and private person—especially in the years of her great fame—Margaret Mitchell created one of fiction's most fiery and flamboyant heroines and one of its most dashing heroes.

Recipient of the National Book Award, The Pulitzer Prize and the adulation of millions of readers throughout the world, Margaret Mitchell kept her remarkable sense of poise and balance, shading the glare of fame's spotlight with her personal reserve and modesty.

This portrait of the author, made at the time of *Gone With the Wind's* early and record-breaking success, captures the depth, dimension, and quiet dignity of her personality.

It is to the memory of that person—whose newspaper career was executed with high style and great humor, a writer whose imagination flourished against the cold facts of history—and of her life—that this work is dedicated—35 years after her death (August 16, 1949).

To a world racked by depression and war, she brought more than a fictional escape into the past. *Gone With the Wind* was for many of its readers a document of survival—a tribute to the tenacity through which man survives.

Stephens Mitchell—tireless executor of his sister's estate—gave unstintingly of his time and talent to the writing and verifying the complete accuracy of this tribute. For the many long interviews; for sharing facts, figures and legal documents from his massive files collected over almost 40 years; and for permission to borrow from his unpublished personal memoir of Margaret Mitchell, we express our deepest thanks.

If generosity is the measure of a man, Stephens Mitchell was a giant. He died in 1983.

Since this book was first published (1974) coauthor Martin Shartar passed away (1982). He was a beloved friend, a man of rare gifts whom the angels graced with extraordinary wit and humanity. His life was music, and everyone he touched will never forget the harmony of his spirit.

– Norman Shavin

THE MILLION DOLLAR LEGENDS:

MARGARET MITCHELL AND "GONE WITH THE WIND"

Courtesy of Lane Brothers Photography

Courtesy of Lane Brothers Photography

"Gone With the Wind" has been translated into more than 24 languages (including Arabic and German). More than 20 million copies have been printed.

A pair of literature's and filmdom's greatest lovers: Rhett (Clark Gable) says farewell to Scarlett (Vivien Leigh) as he leaves to fight in a cause he has insisted is lost.

CONTENTS

CHAPTER I

"SEND THE MANUSCRIPT BACK..."

On an April afternoon in 1935, a reluctant Margaret Mitchell Marsh waited in an Atlanta hotel lobby to keep an appointment with a New York editor. She was 4 feet, 11 inches tall. Beside her were two ragged stacks of manila envelopes reaching almost to her shoulders. They were crammed with the crumbling pages of a manuscript she had started writing nine years before. It was an unfinished novel about the Civil War—many of its pages disfigured by penciled corrections. It had no opening chapter. It had no title.

"I have no novel," she told the editor the day before, when he asked to read it. But John Marsh persuaded her to deliver the untidy manuscript. He had encouraged her in 1926 to begin writing it while she was bedridden, recuperating from a freshly sprained ankle badly weakened by two horseback riding accidents in her youth.

"Take the thing before I change my mind," she told the startled editor. He bought a suitcase to carry the envelopes and left for New Orleans by train.

By that night she changed her mind and telegraphed the editor's New Orleans hotel: "SEND THE MANUSCRIPT BACK, I'VE CHANGED MY MIND."

She was too late.

The editor, Harold Latham, was scouting literary prospects for The Macmillan Company. He had started reading the tattered, untitled, incomplete novel on the train.

Like 20 million other readers who would begin the novel, he couldn't stop.

It became *Gone With the Wind.*

The tiny, modest, soft-spoken author who changed her mind had unknowingly created a giant legend that would enchant the world — and shatter her private life with public acclaim which she neither expected nor wanted.

"GWTW": Danish version

Her most optimistic expectation, she later confided, was $5,000 for the novel begun partly as therapy but which became a challenge of craft and a labor of love. She received a check for $10,500 on July 1, 1936 — 14 months after she had tried to recover her manuscript. That was only the beginning: Two months later she received $43,500; in October, $99,-700. By December, 1936, a record-breaking 1 million copies of *Gone With the Wind* were in print.

Fewer than 40 years after its release, more than 20 million copies had been printed throughout the world; hundreds of thousands of pirated editions were also printed.

David O. Selznick paid $50,000 for the film rights — the highest sum offered for a first novel up to 1936 — even before the novel started its spectacular run to top the best seller lists. It led the list for two years. (In the hectic Summer of her success, she wrote: "I asked the man at the local Macmillan Company [office] if he didn't think I'd be off the list by September and he said I might stay on until Christmas but then publishers are always optimistic.")

Thirty years after its world premiere in Atlanta (1939), the film still is being shown and has grossed more than $100 million.

In May, 1974, NBC contracted to pay $5 million for a one-time telecast, scheduled for 1976.

Margaret Mitchell died August 16, 1949, a few months before her 49th birthday. She was struck five days earlier, while crossing Peachtree Street with her husband to attend a movie, by a speeding car whose driver already had 24 traffic citations.

Except for the novelist's brother Stephens, most of those involved in publishing the novel and creating the film are dead.

Scarlett O'Hara, Rhett Butler, Melnie Hamilton, Ashley Wilkes, Mammy, Prissy and all the other fictional characters still live.

Gone With the Wind is a legend like every fable whose history teases with its networks of tangled chance and circumstance:

Young Margaret absorbing twice-told tales of the Confederacy; the adventuresome child thrown by her horse; the chance-taking newspaper reporter chronicling the Jazz Age; the firsthand experience of panic in the streets of Atlanta during the fire of 1917, of grief in wartime, of the Depression; the loving husband, John Marsh, urging her to write; the friend telling colleagues at Macmillan about a born storyteller; an editor reading tattered pages on a train, ignoring the request to return them; characters animating those pages with their vivid, headstrong lives . . .

These are but a few of the strands that weave the legend of *Gone With the Wind.*

CHAPTER II

THE LADY AND THE LEGEND

Eugene Mitchell, a history-loving attorney who had struggled successfully through the financial crisis of 1893, and his wife Maybelle, a woman so devoted to literature that she paid her children to read, had lost their first child — a son — in infancy. Their second son, Stephens, was four when, on November 8, 1900, Margaret Munnerlyn Mitchell was born and put to crib.

That date does not mark an event as shattering as the San Francisco earthquake or the Chicago fire, but it was the beginning in Atlanta of a legend of more universal dimension. By the time she was 40, Margaret Mitchell and *Gone With the Wind* had made a permanent impact on the publishing and film media, Atlanta— and the world. Her success contributed to changing U.S. income tax laws to benefit writers (and others) and encouraged the United States to participate more fully in world copyright agreements. Her novel alone conquered millions in more than two dozen foreign editions, in Braille and recordings for the blind, in serial form, in paperback. And it created for Atlanta a fictional image as compelling as the history from which it was made.

The alchemy of *Gone With the Wind* enchants almost 40 years after publication by The Macmillan Company, June 30, 1936. By 1973, the novel entered its 82nd American printing, with reported international sales of 20,433,651 copies. Adding the TV revenue, the film will have grossed nearly $125 million. It has already been seen by an estimated 200 million persons. It holds the box office record for single admission sales; the scheduled telecast may attract 50 million viewers.

What accounts for the magic of *Gone With the Wind?*

At its publication, enthusiastic

From the Estate of Margaret Mitchell; courtesy Stephens Mitchell

Maybelle Stephens Mitchell gave her daughter many strengths.

From the Estate of Margaret Mitchell; courtesy Stephens Mitchell

Margaret's father, Eugene Muse Mitchell— an attorney who loved history

critics praised the novel's readability and the author's storytelling gifts. Stephens Mitchell was one of the first to read his sister's novel in its final form.

"It's competent," he said — an understated compliment from an attorney who prizes clarity. And he sustains his original judgment: "The whole thing is just well done. There's not a paragraph in it that can't be understood by the average well-educated high school graduate."

Part of its wide appeal flows from its lean telling of a red-clay real epic. Margaret Mitchell fixed the drama of *Gone With the Wind* by months of exhaustive research, building for her characters a life-true stage.

Yet there are elements beyond a storyteller's charmed pen that have assured *Gone With the Wind* a life longer than most historical novels and a claim stronger on its readers than kindred sagas of love and war, tragedy and defeat, courage and weakness in the maelstrom of history's relentless suck.

Gone With the Wind has all of that and more. In a rare radio broadcast at the time of its publication (at the height of her fame she refused such interviews), Margaret Mitchell said the core of her book is the theme of survival. Throughout history man has struggled with disaster and change, and Margaret had learned from her mother to respect those who survive the worst the world can inflict. Margaret created vivid and vulnerable characters caught in the tumult of shattering change. She inspired her figures with the breath of legend, pulsed them with the urgency of life. Her characters "played the game," as Stephens says, "because they had an inner compulsion to play it out."

Margaret's characters were pure invention. She always insisted, sometimes in letters answering strangers

From the Estate of Margaret Mitchell; courtesy Stephens Mitchell

Margaret and brother Stephens with their mother (circa 1905)

who thought they had recognized relatives in her novel, that none were copied from real life. She laughed when readers claimed kinship with Scarlett or likened the vixen to the author, for Scarlett was less than admirable. When Margaret was described as the autobiographical model for Melanie, she replied: "Being a product of the Jazz Age, being one of those short-haired short-skirted hard-boiled women who preachers said would go to hell or be hanged before they were 30, I am naturally a little embarrassed at finding myself the incarnate spirit of the old South."

Her novel is imbued less with the "spirit of the old South" than with its day-to-day substance. Political issues surrender to the minor particulars of life, ranging from Civil War surgical techniques to the logistics of Confederate manufacture and supply, from what people wore in the 1860s to what they ate and how they spoke. She even checked the temperatures and hours of barbecues and battles. And all these minutiae fleshed the dilemma of a woman "who had a good man but didn't know it until it was too late," as Stephens says of Scarlett's folly of the heart.

The reading public in 1936 was still reeling from the impact of World War I, a worldwide depression, and the dark threat of dictatorships. Readers were ripe for a *Gone With the Wind*. More — they were hungry for an hours-long, day-and-night escape into the rebuilt landscape of a shattered realm.

Margaret transported them through Beauregard's battles and Belle's boudoirs. She climaxed the journey with one of literature's most provocative openings.

Readers could not wait for Scarlett's "Tomorrow." *They* gave a damn. They worried consciously — by telegram, special delivery letter and middle-of-the-night phone call to the fame-harried author — asking "Did Scarlett get Rhett back?"

Readers must have been unconsciously aware of what Margaret identified as her major theme. Courage is a commodity few possess, and Scarlett is *not* courageous. Stephens comments: "She had no courage. She gave way to everything that came along, but she *survived*."

From the Estate of Margaret Mitchell; courtesy Stephens Mitchell

Snapped by a street photographer at 17 months. Brother Stephens says: "She always scowled as an infant."

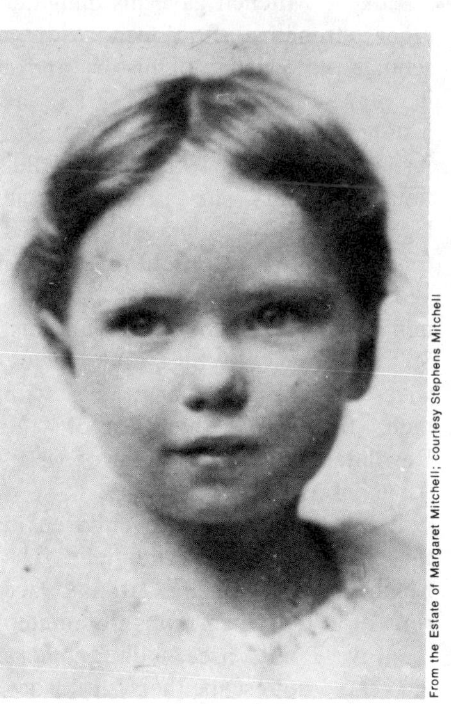
From the Estate of Margaret Mitchell; courtesy Stephens Mitchell

By age three, Margaret was often smiling.

Margaret had mastered her own art of survival — had endured a bad marriage and succeeded with her second husband, John Marsh; had abandoned her faith; had suffered painful accidents — which ironically led to the writing of *Gone With the Wind* — and learned to cope with the relentless pressures of fame.

Her brother remembers her obsession for horses; her passion for riding was such that accidents were no hurdle. "You get badly bunged up with horses," Stephens says, "but if you ride much at all, you'll take a fall."

Margaret *took* her falls and remounted, despite sometimes constant, crippling pain. Her very novel translated history's disastrous falls into

From the Estate of Margaret Mitchell; courtesy Stephens Mitchell

Margaret at 14

understandable terms, telling in bare prose of people who fell but tamed nightmare. She dramatized the difficult business of living to a world already caught in the quickening sands of insanity.

* * *

The year of Margaret's birth — 1900 — enlarges on the legend of *Gone With the Wind*. She described herself as a product of the Jazz Age, a modern woman who rebelled against the shallow customs and conformity of her Time. But she was also shaped by the century just past, filled with its fact and folklore. Her childhood memories included shadowed Sundays nestled on shiny taffetaed laps and stony veterans' knees, absorbing retellings of times not yet out of mind.

She heard first person memories of the Civil War and Reconstruction from those who fought the battles, knew the defeats. As a child she rode horseback with salty-tongued survivors who praised their regiments, echoed their victories, rehearsed their politics, cursed the carpetbaggers. She memorized Atlanta's Cyclorama, roamed Kennesaw Mountain breastworks, dug Minié balls.

She visited the Jonesboro farm of her spinster great-aunts, Mary and Sarah Fitzgerald. She rode by carriage with her mother through Clayton County — destined to become Tara's domain. She saw the chimneys of torched houses: "Sherman's sentinels" her mother called them.

In her thirties, Margaret recalled the hot September day when her mother drove her — then six — down the road to Jonesboro: "[She] showed me the old ruins of houses where fine and wealthy people had once lived. Some of the ruins dated from Sherman's visit, some had fallen to pieces when the families in them fell to pieces. And she showed me plenty of houses still standing staunchly.

"And she talked about the world those people had lived in, such a secure world, and how it had exploded beneath them. And she told me that my own world was going to explode under me, some day, and God help me if I didn't have some weapon to meet the new world. She was talking about the necessity of having an education, both classical and practical. For she said that all that would be left after a world ended would be what you could do with your hands and what you had in your head."

From her mother, Maybelle Stephens Mitchell, came Irish pride and independence, an allegiance to custom and courage. A devout Roman Catholic in a predominantly Protestant society, a suffragette who took her daughter to rallies, Mrs. Mitchell exemplied the strength-in-grace ingrained within the author.

Eugene Mitchell gave his daughter other strengths. Equipped with a scholar's knowledge of history and a lawyer's appreciation of order, he instilled a respect for clarity, fact and justice. Descended from pre-Revolutionary settlers, he preserved the legacy of family history and repeated to his children stories of pioneering Scotsmen and women — lawyers, ministers, Huguenot immigrants, Stuart refugees, Whigs and Tories; wives who settled alien places with their husbands; veterans of the Revolutionary War, the War of 1812, the Civil War.

He instructed the two children in the challenges of the moment. The Mitchells witnessed the Atlanta race riots of 1906, when mobs dominated the Five Points area, killing blacks who could not escape their fury. They saw the angry rioters of 1916 who protested Gov. John M. Slaton's commutation of Leo Frank's death sentence for the alleged rape-slaying of a young girl. Frank was Jewish, and Stephens Mitchell remembers the rabble-rousers who caused the lynching of Frank. Stephens says of his father's respect for Gov. Slaton, a longtime friend: "People who stood by order in that day, when it was difficult and dangerous to do so, stood by order all of their lives. It was a religion to them. It was a religion to Margaret . . ."

Margaret shared even more with Stephens. Their close relationship lasted throughout her life. Among Stephens' memories is her youthful ability to captivate an audience with stories culled from her avid reading and her rich imagining.

And there was the love of horses. Margaret and Stephens bought a pony with their own savings, trading it later for a horse they named "Bucephalus," after the steed of Alexander the Great. The two serious injuries, in 1911 and 1920, remind Stephens of the deaths of Bonnie Blue Butler and Gerald O'Hara in *Gone With the Wind*.

Ghost stories she told to the frightened delight of companions became drawing room theatricals with the young playwright portraying heroes as well as heroines. Reading fired Margaret's mind: the whole of

From the Estate of Margaret Mitchell; courtesy Stephens Mitchell

Teenage Margaret strikes dramatically defiant pose.

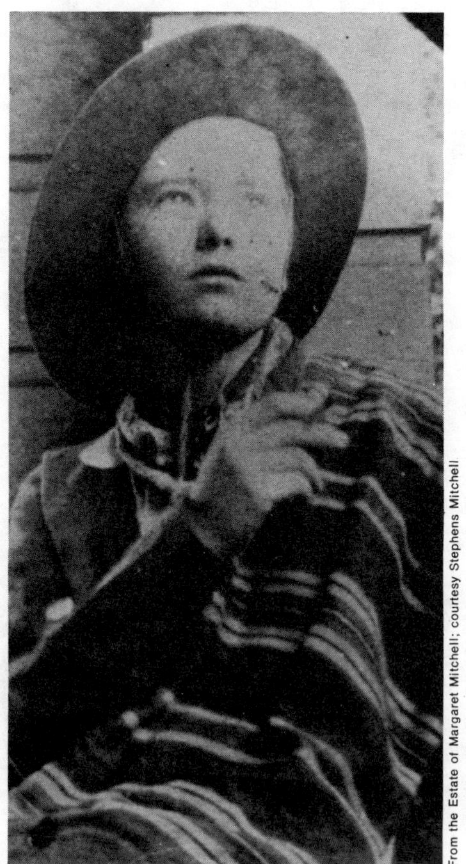

From the Estate of Margaret Mitchell; courtesy Stephens Mitchell

In costume for one of her early plays

From the Estate of Margaret Mitchell; courtesy Stephens Mitchell

As Steve Hoyle in her play "The Traitor"

Shakespeare, the novels of Sir Walter Scott and Charles Dickens.

Her parents paid her small sums for each work she read. When *Gone With the Wind* was compared favorably to Tolstoi's *War and Peace* and Thackery's *Vanity Fair* she recalled: "Most of my 'classical' reading was done before the age of 12, aided by five, 10 and 15 cents a copy bribes from my father and abetted by the hair brush or mother's number three slipper. She just about beat the hide off of me for not reading Tolstoi or Thackery or Jane Austen — but I preferred to be beaten."

As a teenager, she began writing stories, mostly tales of adventure about bandits, frontiersmen, and brave young women. Stephens remembers breadboxes filled with stories "written in pencil on little school tablets — stories, plays, skits, jokes . . . but mainly stories."

As a student at Atlanta's Washington Seminary, a private school for girls, Margaret continued to write. In 1917 the school annual published "Little Sister," her narrative bustling with bandits, murder, pillage, rape. Its heroine was Peggy — the name Margaret used during her newspaper career in the Twenties.

The world was at war during Margaret's school years, and in 1917, her senior year, the United States entered World War I. That Spring, Atlanta suffered a Sherman-like fire that ravaged 20 residential blocks. Municipal Auditorium (later the scene of festivities celebrating the world premiere of the film *Gone With the Wind*) was an emergency center for terrified refugees. Margaret was a volunteer, witness to the confusion that her novel stitches with needle-sharp intensity as Atlanta falls while Scarlett struggles toward Tara.

Her teenage years brought more heart-bruising encounters with personal grief. In 1918, when she enrolled at Smith College (Northampton, Mass.) to study medicine, she became engaged to Lt. Clifford Henry, who had been stationed at Camp Gordon (Chamblee, Ga.). He was wounded in action in October and awarded the Croix de Guerre at the hospital where he died days before the Armistice.

From the Estate of Margaret Mitchell; courtesy Stephens Mitchell

Margaret at the beach in 1916

The next year Margaret's mother died during the national influenza epidemic.

If these tragedies summon episodes from *Gone With the Wind,* they are further testament to her agile refinement of the stuff of existence into the strands of fiction.

After her mother's death, Margaret quit school to return home to keep house and serve as hostess for her father.

From the Estate of Margaret Mitchell; courtesy Stephens Mitchell

School annual published story in her senior year.

From the Estate of Margaret Mitchell; courtesy Stephens Mitchell

Her ready smile became a trademark.

From the Estate of Margaret Mitchell; courtesy Stephens Mitchell

Even when casual, she could be dramatic.

In 1920, there was her second horseback accident.

Determined that his daughter not be a housebound attendant, Eugene Mitchell introduced her to society through Atlanta's Debutante Club.

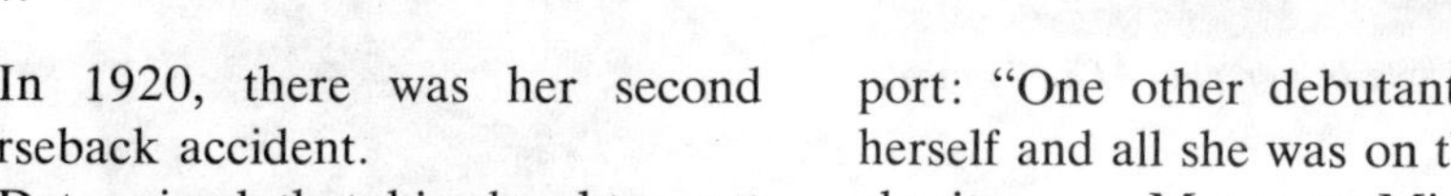

Margaret, debutante at 20, startling Atlanta's old-line doyennes with her daring Apache dance, is not the newly widowed Scarlett scandalizing the Atlanta Bazaar (though today's readers of *Gone With the Wind* would appreciate the irony, half a century after that fictional event, of *The Atlanta Constitution's* society page report: "One other debutante offering herself and all she was on the altar of charity . . . Margaret Mitchell, you know.").

As Stephens recalls, everyone knew Margaret was "about the best dancer of her crowd," earning at times a spotlighted display of exhibition ballroom dancing. A newspaper photo of Margaret posed on a locomotive confirms that she was good copy partly because of her beauty.

In Atlanta society, Debutante Club membership usually led to Junior League acceptance, a provincial Peachtree Street equivalent of Philadelphia Main Line status. Miss Margaret Munnerlyn Mitchell was not invited to join.

The rebuff apparently did little more than remind her of traditional social pecking orders, giving her novel yet another degree of authenticity when Rhett Butler begins to prepare Bonnie Blue for social acceptance while she is still in her pram.

On September 2, 1922, Margaret married Berrien Kinnard Upshaw against her family's wishes. The newlyweds lived in the Mitchells'

From the Estate of Margaret Mitchell; courtesy Stephens Mitchell

Roughing it on a camping trip

From the Estate of Margaret Mitchell; courtesy Stephens Mitchell

Dressed for a hike at age 18

Wistful debutante faces the Twenties. Cat is another trademark.

From the Estate of Margaret Mitchell; courtesy Stephens Mitchell

Peachtree Street home. Before the end of that year, Upshaw left Margaret and Atlanta. She was relieved. Some who knew him describe Upshaw as highly unstable, though details of his life are scant. Fourteen years later, when she received threatening letters from Upshaw after she became famous, Margaret kept a revolver near her bedside until informed of his death.

The best man in her marriage to Upshaw was John Marsh, former English teacher, then employed as a copy editor for *The Atlanta Georgian;* he soon joined the staff of *The Atlanta Journal.*

Stephens remarks that Margaret had been "tempered by the world": the deaths of Lt. Henry and her mother; the selfless withdrawal from college; the rejection by the Junior League; the unfortunate marriage; the inexplicable abandonment of her religion.

But like the characters in her novel, she had learned to play out the game of being alive and to play it well.

A refreshing pause

From the Estate of Margaret Mitchell; courtesy Stephens Mitchell

At Stone Mountain in 1922

From the Estate of Margaret Mitchell; courtesy Stephens Mitchell

CHAPTER III
JAZZ AGE JOURNALIST

In December, 1922, about the time Upshaw disappeared, Margaret joined *The Atlanta Journal Sunday Magazine,* the weekly supplement whose staff had included Don Marquis, Erskine Caldwell, Ward Morehouse, Grantland Rice, Laurence Stallings and Lamar Trotti.

Neither Angus Perkerson, the Magazine's editor, nor his wife, novelist Medora Field Perkerson, could have known that the 22-year-old who wrote under the by-line Peggy Upshaw (she soon changed it to Peggy Mitchell) would become best known of the Magazine's alumni. They learned that an ex-debutante could be a sparkling, witty writer: Her gifted intelligence, command of language, and knack for distilling the grain of a story were already evident.

Peggy Mitchell's salary was $25 a week (later $30); her assignments were more rewarding. Her literate conversational agility embellished her interviews with Rudolph Valentino (she referred to The Sheik's "soft sibilant accent"), Mrs. Rebecca Latimer Felton (first woman U.S. Senator), Tiger Flowers (1926 middleweight boxing champion), Harry K. Thaw (notorious for having shot Stanford White; she described Thaw's hair as the "gray of a Maltese cat"), and Gutzon Borglum (the sculptor of Mount Rushmore who was first commissioned to carve the Confederate Memorial across the face of Stone Mountain).

For the Borglum interview she donned coveralls and was suspended in a bosun's chair used for the carving. For a photo accompanying a circus article, she was hoisted by trunk atop an elephant.

From the Estate of Margaret Mitchell; courtesy Stephens Mitchell

With friend Augusta Dearborn (left) in front of Mitchells' Peachtree Street home

From the Estate of Margaret Mitchell; courtesy Stephens Mitchell

Photographed by John Marsh in 1922

From the Estate of Margaret Mitchell; courtesy Stephens Mitchell

Apache dance startled Atlanta socialites.

Courtesy Atlanta Journal-Constitution Sunday Magazine

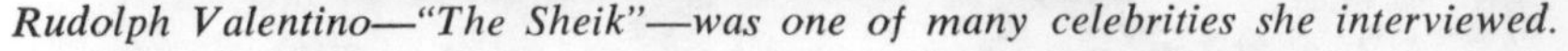

Rudolph Valentino—"The Sheik"—was one of many celebrities she interviewed.

Courtesy Atlanta Journal-Constitution Sunday Magazine

In bosun's chair used for Stone Mountain carving

The scrapbook of her articles bulged with 139 stories, 89 signed with her by-line. In 1936, she shared a rare self-assessment of her work: "I'm not a stylist, God knows, and couldn't be if I tried. Moreover, I sweat blood to keep my style as bare as a law report, as unadorned as the newspaper versions of a hit-and-run accident."

The early to mid-Twenties were for Margaret as happy as they were busy. "The things that most influenced us were automobiles, music, dancing," Stephens reminisces. And he enumerates the writers who stoked Margaret's insatiable appetite for words: James Branch Cabell (her choice among "stylists"), Joseph Hergesheimer, Stephen Vincent Benét, Ellen Glasgow, Willa Cather, and F. Scott Fitzgerald. (During her great fame she visited Benét, Cabell and Glasgow, among other prominent writers. Fitzgerald worked briefly on Sidney Howard's screenplay of *Gone With the Wind.)*

Margaret read, wrote, and reveled

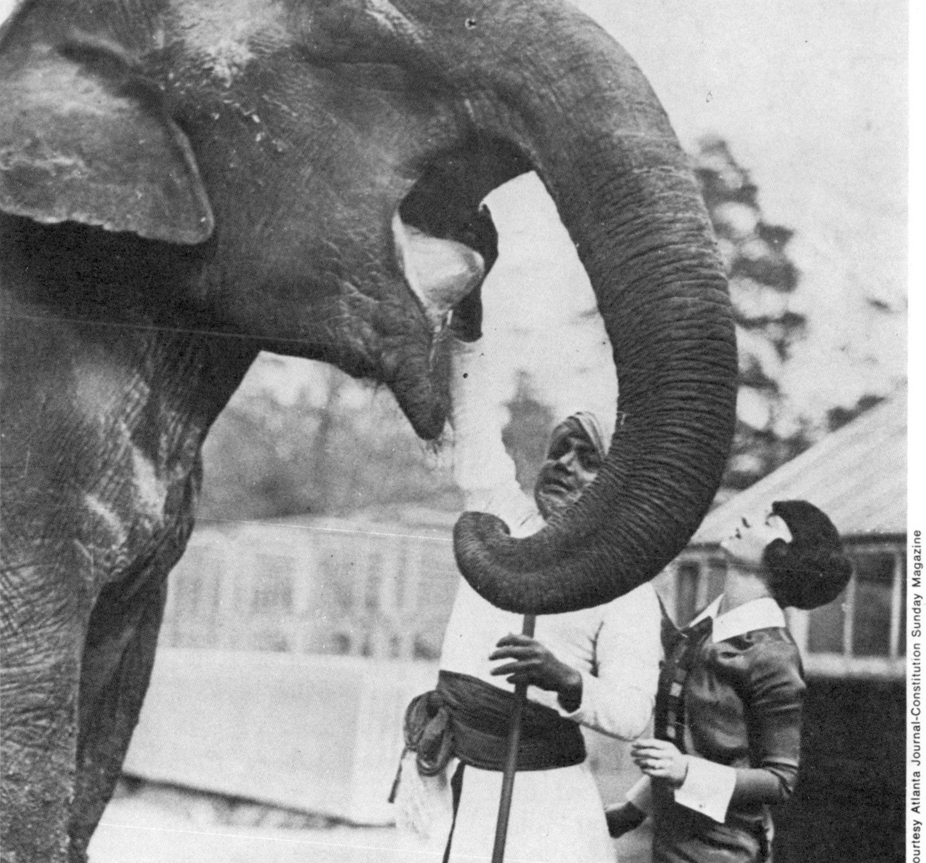

Courtesy Atlanta Journal-Constitution Sunday Magazine

Interviewing animal trainer. Elephant's trunk lifted her to animal's head.

Courtesy Atlanta Journal-Constitution Sunday Magazine

Aggressive reporter pursued subject in an elevator.

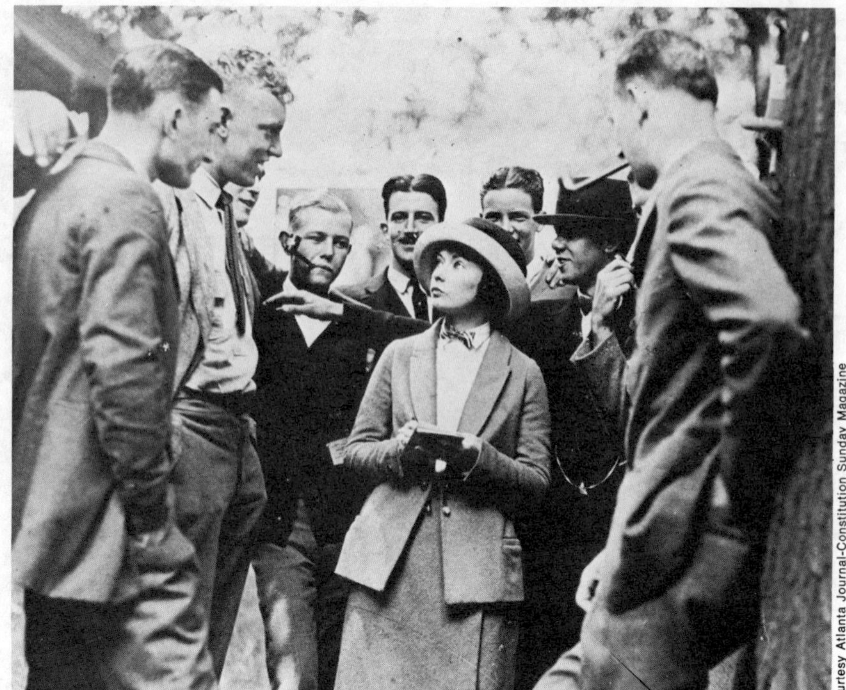

Courtesy Atlanta Journal-Constitution Sunday Magazine

Like Scarlett at barbecue, Margaret was surrounded by collegiates; here she interviewed Tech students.

Courtesy Atlanta Journal-Constitution Sunday Magazine

Young reporter frequently posed for illustrations to accompany her articles.

in films; Chaplin and the Marx Brothers delighted her. She entered a social milieu different from upper-case Atlanta Society. She joined a galaxy of talented writers and artists who were anti-Puritan, anti-Prohibition, and anti-Ku Klux Klan. She associated with "The Peachtree Yacht Club." Stephens calls this "a drinking club," justifying its name in a city without ships: "There are no athletes at the Athletic Club and no one drives at the Driving Club. Why should there be yachts at the Yacht Club?"

Included in Margaret's literary circle was John Marsh, who had left *The Atlanta Journal* to join the Georgia Power Company's advertising and publicity department.

John and Margaret grew close. Before 1924 ended, Margaret Mitchell Upshaw was granted an uncontested divorce.

CHAPTER IV

THE BIRTH OF A BEST SELLER

Nationally, it was the year of the flapper, *The Great Gatsby* and bathtub gin.

In Georgia, it was the year of bootleg, the boll weevil and faltering banks.

On Independence Day, 1925, Margaret Mitchell and John Marsh were married.

They rented a small apartment on Crescent Avenue, a block from Peachtree Street — destined to become creatively and tragically prominent in Margaret's life.

On the door were two calling cards: "Mr. John R. Marsh" and "Miss Margaret Munnerlyn Mitchell." The gesture was daring for 1925, but was not unusual for the woman who was about to create one of fiction's most fiercely independent heroines.

Heroes and heroines — fictional and historical — occupied much of her time. Her *Journal Sunday Magazine* assignments included profiles of the several Confederate heroes planned for inclusion in the Stone Mountain Memorial carving. (The finished sculpture depicts only President Jefferson Davis and Generals Robert E. Lee and Thomas J. "Stonewall" Jackson.) Her essays reflected knowledge of the period, flair for vivid portraiture, and thoroughness of research.

Margaret was also writing fiction.

In May, 1926, she left the Magazine, though she continued to contribute anecdotes. In the Fall of the year she sprained the ankle first injured in childhood and weakened by the 1920 riding accident. She spent weeks in a cast, then more weeks in traction and on crutches.

During her convalescence she read more voraciously than usual. As an antidote to the tedium of confinement — and because he knew her ability — John Marsh encouraged his wife to write a novel. It was started before the end of 1926, written in random order, last chapter first.

From the Estate of Margaret Mitchell; courtesy Stephens Mitchell

The Jazz Age begins, and Margaret captures its beat.

Friends knew that an expanding manuscript was being developed in the Crescent Avenue apartment. Affectionately nicknamed "The Dump," the apartment was a gathering place for the couple's literate friends. Large parties alternated with evenings devoted to conversation and occasional charades.

Stephens describes the group that formed about Margaret and John in their apartment: "All of them . . . were interested in the new day" that had been hinted might dawn. "We were interested in politics about Prohibition . . . We were readers of *The American Mercury* and followed whatever H. L. Mencken and George Jean Nathan wrote . . . We took up for Negroes, who were much oppressed by the local police of that day. We believed in freedom of speech and writing. There was much talk, and many cigarettes were smoked, and ideas were built up and torn down."

But there was the other, more 19th Century aspect of Margaret's personality: the reserved and reticent woman who would find world acclaim uncomfortable. Though friends knew there was a work in progress— afternoon callers saw pages piling up at her desk — she shared the manuscript only with her husband.

Among her frequent visitors was Lois Cole, a friend employed in the Atlanta office of The Macmillan Company. Margaret was secretive about her novel even to Lois Cole, who suggested it be submitted to Macmillan. Margaret disparaged it as a work no one would want to see.

The novel was virtually complete by 1929. It still lacked an opening chapter, a few transitional passages, was untitled, and within a few years it was stored in a closet.

In 1932, the Marshes left "The Dump" for more comfortable quarters on Seventeenth Street. That year Lois Cole, married to Allan Taylor, left Atlanta to become an associate editor at Macmillan's New York office. The following year she wrote Margaret a formal invitation to submit her manuscript. The author refused, saying it was incomplete and repeating that no one would be interested in reading it. After the novel's publication she wrote: "I never ex-

Margaret and father examine first copy of "Gone With the Wind." His appraisal: "A work of genius."

pected to sell my book and didn't write it to sell but only to amuse and occupy myself while on crutches."

The Marshes continued their placid life among friends in a city that maintained a kind of grace even in the Depression. Because of John Marsh's position with the Georgia Power Company, the couple was relatively secure, but *Gone With the Wind's* accurate rendering of the difficult 1860s was written against the author's firsthand observation of the tormented Twenties. It was another time of testing, a challenge not to go under in the whirl of events.

In 1934 Margaret was injured again. Her spine jolted in an auto collision, she wore a brace for months; years later she would undergo corrective surgery, which was unsuccessful.

In 1934 other events were knitting into the stuff of legend from which the massive novel would be woven. Georgia-born novelist Caroline Miller's *Lamb In His Bosom* was awarded the Pulitzer Prize for fiction (it is a story of back-country life in pre-Civil War Georgia), and by the end of 1934 The Macmillan Company decided to discover American talent.

Harold Latham was editor-in-chief of Macmillan's trade department; his British scouting forays produced successes such as Richard Llewellyn's *How Green Was My Valley*. He undertook his American literary expedition in the Spring of 1935. Atlanta was the first stop on a tour from the South to the Pacific. Lois Cole, his associate at Macmillan, mentioned Margaret's manuscript to Latham, commenting that only John Marsh had read it, but adding that if the author could write "the way she talks, it should be a honey of a book." She also wrote Medora Field Perkerson asking her to make Latham's visit as pleasant as possible.

Mrs. Perkerson arranged a luncheon where Latham was introduced to Margaret. Mrs. Perkerson confirmed the report that Margaret had written a novel. When he asked to see the manuscript, Margaret answered that she had no novel to show but promised if she ever finished it she would offer it first to Macmillan.

John Marsh persuaded her to change her mind, and Margaret delivered the mound of aging envelopes to Latham's hotel as he was about to leave Atlanta for New Orleans. Meeting the diminutive author in the lobby, Latham faced the biggest manuscript he'd ever seen. Margaret urged him to take "the thing" before she changed her mind. Latham did—buying a suitcase to carry the stacks of yellowing pages.

Margaret was only 4 feet 11 inches tall, but once said, "I don't *feel* small . . . I feel myself as big as anyone else and twice as strong." Apparently still unaware that she had given the editor a literally larger-than-life manuscript, hours later her strength ebbed sufficiently to telegraph his New Orleans hotel: "SEND THE MANUSCRIPT BACK, I'VE CHANGED MY MIND."

But Harold Latham had started to read the novel en route to New Orleans. He ignored her cable, reading the work as he traveled across the country. His New York associates agreed with his estimate of the novel, and Macmillan offered Margaret a contract if she would finish it.

In July, she received their official offer: a royalty of 10 per cent of the retail price of the first 10,000 copies sold, 15 per cent thereafter, and a $500 advance against royalties (half on signing, half on delivery of a completed manuscript).

The condition of the manuscript—yellowed pages full of penciled corrections; the awkward transitions, the

Courtesy of Lane Brothers Photography

"GWTW": Swedish edition

missing first chapter, the absence of a satisfactory title — all these factors must have prompted Margaret's comment to her husband that she didn't see how Macmillan "could make heads or tails of it." After her success, she admitted: "In my wildest imaginings I didn't believe that that old mess of copypaper which hung around the house so many years, which I didn't think even worth re-typing and sending off, would ever make the best seller lists. And I'm flabbergasted."

She accepted the publisher's offer, committing herself to six months of exhausting effort—polishing, tightening, checking for accuracy, making certain her fictional names *were* fictional. (Only after her book had gone to press did she learn of the appointment of Father Gerald P. O'Hara as Bishop of the newly formed Roman Catholic Diocese of Savannah-Atlanta. After publication she wrote him an apology for any embarrassment the coincidence might cause, pointing out that Macmillan could not afford the time to reset her character's name when she learned of the Bishop's appointment.)

Other changes were made, however, between the draft and the finished text. Her heroine's name was more vividly and memorably changed from Pansy to Scarlett; Fontenoy Hall became Tara. The problem of choosing a title remained.

The book's closing line yielded *Tomorrow Is Another Day* as a possibility, but Margaret discovered that 46 books with "tomorrow" in their titles had been published, 13 of them still in print. Macmillan accepted *Another Day* as a title, but the author, still dissatisfied, submitted more than 50 alternates. They included *Ba! Ba! Black Sheep* and *Tote The Weary Load,* and, from a Confederate poem, *Bugles Sang True.*

Among the suggested titles was a phrase preferred by the novelist. She found it in the 19th Century poet Ernest Dowson's *Cynara:*

I have forgot much, Cynara! gone with the wind,
Flung roses, roses riotously with the throng,
Dancing, to put thy pale, lost lilies out of mind;
But I was desolate and sick of an old passion,
Yea, all the time, because the dance was long:
I have been faithful to thee, Cynara! in my fashion.

It was pure coincidence that in the 24th chapter of her novel Scarlett muses: "Was Tara still standing? Or was Tara also gone with the wind which had swept through Georgia?"

Macmillan enthusiastically accepted the title. Though the poem and the novel are not thematic kin, Margaret must have recognized not only that "gone with the wind" conveyed the sweeping change that structured her story, but also that the poem's references to "an old passion" appropriately echoed the tangled emotions ensnaring her principal characters.

Scarlett O'Hara is caught in the cadence of a dance, forced by the winds of chance to choreograph her own destiny. And Margaret Mitchell was about to be drawn into a dance whose frenzy she could not have guessed. *Gone With the Wind* was about to become a lucrative — and intricate — international enterprise absorbing the Marshes and Stephens Mitchell in matters ranging from world copyright laws to the sale of film rights, and even what to do about Al Capp's parody of the characters in his *Li'l Abner* comic strip.

Legal entanglements began almost immediately after final copy was delivered to Macmillan in February, 1936. Pleading the high cost of publishing a 1,037 page book (despite the writer's offers to shorten it), Macmillan adjusted the contract, offering 15 per cent royalty on sales above 25,000 copies.

By April, British rights were secured by Macmillan & Co. Ltd. of London. Shortly thereafter, the Book of the Month Club chose the novel as its July selection, and Macmillan postponed the release from May 31 to June 30. During July, 100,000 copies were printed. By Christmas, 1936, a million copies had been printed, priced at $3.

One myth about *Gone With the Wind* is that it succeeded despite negative criticism. In fact, however, readers were lured by lavish reviews. *The New York Times* and *The New York Herald Tribune* devoted the front pages of their July 5th book review sections to the novel. J. Donald Adams headlined his *Times* appraisal, "A Fine Novel of the Civil War," calling it "one of the most remarkable first novels produced by an American writer" and "one of the best . . . in sheer readability, surpassed by nothing in American fiction." Adams hedged his praise by not ranking *Gone With the Wind* among the masterpieces of all time, but what he called its "sheer readability" became the key phrase in most reviews, even the few unfavorable ones. He ended with: "It is a

Courtesy of Lane Brothers Photography

"GWTW": German edition

book of uncommon quality, a superb piece of story-telling which nobody who finds pleasure in the art of fiction can afford to neglect."

The *Tribune's* reviewer, widely respected historian Henry Steele Commager, praised the novel's sincerity, passion and understanding, and said it was "woven of the stuff of history and of disciplined imagination . . . a dramatic recreation of life itself."

Stephen Vincent Benét, author of *John Brown's Body,* wrote in *Saturday Review of Literature* that the novel was original and exciting, hailing it as "a solid and vividly interesting story of war and reconstruction, realistic in detail . . ."

Margaret had expressed concern about the novel's potential reception in the South, but reviewers in Atlanta and other Southern cities added their enthusiastic comments to the national torrent of praise.

Negative comments were typified by Louis Kronenberger's reservations in *The New Yorker.* He began with praise: "For sheer readability I can think of nothing it must give way before; with her first novel, Miss Mitchell proves herself to be a staggeringly gifted storyteller, empowered, as it were, with some secretion in the blood for effortlessly inventing and prolonging excitement . . ." But he then called it "a masterpiece of pure escapism," concluding: "It provides a kind of catharsis, not, to be sure, of pity and terror, but rather of all the false sentiment and heady goo that even the austerest mind somehow accumulates."

Malcolm Cowley's assessment in *The New Republic* complained that the novel glorified "the plantation legend," prompting his colleague Stark Young (author of the Civil War novel *So Red The Rose)* to write Margaret a letter disagreeing with Cowley. She answered that praise from "the Left Wingers" would have mortified her:

"I'd have to do so much explaining to family and friends if the aesthetes and radicals of literature liked it . . . One and all they have savaged me and given me great pleasure. However, I wish some of

Courtesy of Lane Brothers Photography

Dutch version: first edition

them would actually read the book and review the book I wrote — not the book they imagine I've written or the book they think I should have written."

Margaret never considered herself a great novelist or a gifted stylist, yet she must have been gratified by praise from writers such as Benét, Commager, Ellen Glasgow, Du Bose Heyward, Storm Jameson, Kathleen Norris and Sterling North.

During the first year of publication *Gone With the Wind* grossed close to $3 million and saved a number of Depression-ravaged book stores. It was the first $3 best seller and topped the lists for two consecutive years. Average daily sales neared 4,000 copies; a New York bookstore placed an order for 5,000 copies. (When Macmillan accepted the novel, Margaret confided to her husband, "I still don't see how they expect to sell any copies." He answered, "Don't worry about that. You and I have so many cousins, we'll sell at least 5,000 copies in Georgia alone.")

In 1937, *Gone With the Wind* received the American Booksellers Association's annual award (now The National Book Awards) and the Pulitzer Prize for fiction. It eclipsed other titles published in 1936, including Pearl Buck's *The Exile,* Aldous Huxley's *Eyeless in Gaza,* John Dos Passos' *The Big Money,* George Santayana's *The Last Puritan,* Daphne du Maurier's *Jamaica Inn,* and Walter D. Edmonds' *Drums Along the Mohawk.* The last two were adapted eventually into successful films, but news that screen rights to *Gone With the Wind* were bought by David O. Selznick electrified the nation. Its purchase price of $50,000 — the highest sum paid up to that time for a first novel — paled alongside the national pastime of suggesting a cast. (When Selznick and John Hay Whitney liquidated Selznick International Pictures in 1942, they sent Margaret an additional $50,000 as a token of esteem.)

Selznick launched a highly publicized search for an actress to play Scarlett, but Margaret would be spared the Hollywood machinations that finally brought her book to the screen — though she was bombarded by Selznick seeking assistance. She was forced to insist to the producer: "In issuing instructions to your organization, it ought not to be difficult to make clear what my position is. It is simply that I wrote the book, *and that is all.* I am responsible for my book but I am not responsible for the motion picture. My connection with the motion picture ended on July 30, 1936, when I signed the contract selling you the film rights. I sold them to you lock, stock and barrel and from that day forward they have been yours, to do with as you please."

She tasted the further torment of the less-than-palatable aspects of prominence. She was an international figure, even part of the Hollywood vocabulary. She had to cope with such nuisances as a Louella Parsons gossip column item that she was going blind.

The exhaustive efforts of bringing *Gone With the Wind* to press took their toll. Though not blind, Margaret suffered corneal hemorrhages requiring complete rest and seclusion.

For six months she had labored to shape her unruly manuscript into its final form; John Marsh had taken a two month vacation to help her. It took Selznick — and more than a dozen other writers — longer than two years to achieve a workable script.

Margaret described the first two years following publication of *Gone With the Wind* as "months of torment mixed with joy beyond comprehension." The joy *and* the torment are understandable.

Gone With the Wind had made publishing history. Worldwide sales had already approached 1.5 million in two years. In addition to the Pulitzer Prize and the National Book Award, she received awards from the Florida Library Association and the New York Southern Society. Transactions with European publishers forced her to become an international businesswoman. In 1938, her name appeared in the English edition of *Who's Who* — she was an international celebrity as well.

Stephens remarks that she enjoyed success, savored "being on top of the world," but that she did not enjoy being pointed out like a zoo animal or "being gawked at like Stone Mountain."

During the hectic weeks after the novel's meteoric success she wrote a friend: "My one aim in life at present is to get back to my old quiet life." Her wish was not granted.

The pinnacle of fame was as dizzying for Margaret as were physical heights. She suffered nausea in high places. During the initial whirl of *Gone With the Wind's* acclaim, she was forced to curtail a vacation at Blowing Rock, N.C. She returned to the vertigoes of ceaseless queries.

Margaret was deluged with requests from publishers begging for manuscripts — she refused King Features Syndicate's offer of $1 million for comic strip rights — invitations to lecture, appear on radio, endorse products, travel, and collaborate on surefire sequels. (Stephens summarizes one memorable suggestion made to her: "Rhett Butler has seen the light and is a Baptist evangelist. Belle Watling has reformed and is at Tara as a governess for the children.")

There was a flood of letters (one addressed "MM - GWTW - ATLANTA" was delivered) most of which she felt compelled to answer from ingrained courtesy, especially if the correspondent struck a responsive chord or stimulated her interest in history. Other letters ranged from marriage proposals to pleas for money and attempts to establish kinship, however remote.

Her phone became a relentless demon, bedeviling her with strangers wanting only to talk to the author of *Gone With the Wind,* ask a favor, or endorse an elaborate scheme. A Midwesterner announced she had come to Atlanta solely to be photographed with Margaret and insisted that she would not leave without it.

Impostors appeared everywhere, as many as five in five different cities in the same week. Most were harmless, like the pseudo-Margaret Mitchells who autographed copies of the novel in bookstores or the woman in a Manhattan hotel lobby telling listeners she had written the book at a table in the hotel's restaurant. Others were embarrassing: a drunk at Miami Airport demanded a chartered plane to the Caribbean; an impostor in Los Angeles charged more than $1,000 worth of clothes; another rode between New York and Washington assuring the train's club car occupants that *she* was the author, cadging drinks and flirting with men as she did so.

Courtesy of Lane Brothers Photography

Another Dutch version—this one reflecting the Dutch Supreme Court's ruling in the author's favor

Meanwhile, the real Margaret Mitchell was battling fame. "I'm on the run," she wrote after the book's wild reception. "I'm sure Scarlett O'Hara never struggled to get out of Atlanta or suffered more during the siege of Atlanta than I have suffered during the siege that has been on since publication day."

She could not have foreseen the lawsuits: One was brought against her and Macmillan by an obscure author of a history of the Ku Klux Klan, accusing Margaret of plagiarism because, among other coincidences, both books were bound in "Confederate grey" and *Gone With the Wind* referred to Jefferson Davis and Charleston. She asked $6.5 *billion* in damages; the suit was dismissed. The author sued Billy Rose for staging a musical adaptation of the novel; she settled for $3,000 damages, and Rose apologized.

Despite the verbal agreement with Selznick that she would not be involved in making the film, she was plagued by memos and telegrams from him, his studio, and MGM's publicity department. Playwright Sidney Howard, assigned to fashion the screenplay, wrote for the author's help with Negro dialect; Selznick urgently requested how Mammy's bandana should be tied. Margaret refused to be involved, answering: "I don't know, and I'm not going out on a limb over a headrag."

Out of the painfully learned wisdom that fame is as difficult as notoriety, Margaret avoided any connection with the film. Letting Hollywood handle the transformation of *Gone With the Wind,* she reserved her comments until after the premiere.

Translating *Gone With the Wind* from page to screen required 1 million hours in preparation and production. More than 70 hours of film were edited to 3 hours 40 minutes showing time.

Without a complete cast, without an actress to play Scarlett, Selznick started filming with the fall of Atlanta.

It was a fiery beginning for one of Hollywood's most spectacular hits.

CHAPTER V

"GONE WITH THE WIND" GOES HOLLYWOOD

A wagon is silhouetted against sheets of flame that signal Atlanta's doom. The wagon's occupants are showered with sparks as they flee the fallen city.

The night is not September 1, 1864, but December 10, 1938. The flaming warehouses are not on Atlanta's Marietta Street; they are on a Culver City set. The holocaust is fed by gas-soaked remnants of scenery used in *King Kong, The Garden of Allah* and *The Last of the Mohicans,* rebuilt to resemble crumbling Atlanta.

The wagon's occupants are Rhett, Scarlett, Melanie, her newborn child, and Prissy. Only Scarlett and Rhett are visible, but the actors are stunt men — Clark Gable's contract with MGM does not release him for two months. After two years of tantalizing talent scouting (cost estimated at $92,000), Scarlett is still not cast.

The recreated ruining of Atlanta, delayed by producer David O. Selznick because his brother Myron's party had not arrived to join spectators at the scene, caused a few frightened residents to flee toward the desert. Myron Selznick, a talent agent, arrives as the flames wane; his party includes a young British actress not well known in America. "I want you to meet your Scarlett O'Hara," he says. So ended the search that Selznick had exploited for years. Vivien Leigh became Scarlett.

The casting of *Gone With the Wind* was often front page news, sharing space with the crisis erupting in Europe. Actresses and actors maneuvered for, or tried to avoid, the leading roles; newspaper references to possible stars were given the significance of politicians announcing for office. Women's clubs, chapters of the United Daughters of the Confederacy, columnists, letter-writers by the thousands played the *"GWTW"* guessing game.

The craze started when Katharine (Kay) Brown, an East Coast story editor for Selznick International Pictures, read an advance copy of the novel. She shared passages by phone with Ronald Colman, under contract to Selznick. "Ripping" and "Topping," Colman said, though he admitted to fan magazines urging him as Rhett that Clark Gable was better for the part. Selznick received a reported 75,000 letters demanding

Burning warehouses create one of film's most dramatic scenes, the first to be shot by Selznick. Clark Gable's stand-in, Yakima Canutt, is at left; unidentified stunt man played Scarlett (Vivien Leigh had not yet been cast).

Gable be cast. Alarmed at the flood of support, Gable thought Rhett Butler "too big an order" and claimed not to "want any part of him."

Kay Brown's message to Selznick, accompanying a synopsis of the novel, enthusiastically commended: "I beg, urge, coax and plead with you to read this at once. I know that after you read the book you will drop everything and buy it."

Selznick hesitated. It was a Book of the Month Club selection, Macmillan was mounting a massive promotion, and trade journals were predicting a best seller was about to be born. But *So Red The Rose,* a movie of the Civil War, had bombed at the box office the preceding year.

"Most sorry to have to say no in face of your enthusiasm for this story," Selznick answered Kay Brown.

Selznick had second thoughts. The potential film could be a pioneer color effort for his studio; Gary Cooper might be good as Rhett. "Were I with MGM, I believe I would buy it now for some such combination as Gable and Joan Crawford," said Selznick.

Two days later, other thoughts: Selznick suggested a one week option, considered Colman and Miriam Hopkins or Tallulah Bankhead for the leads.

Six weeks passed. Kay Brown sent a synopsis to John Hay (Jock) Whitney, Chairman of Whitney Enterprises, backers of Selznick's film company. He wanted the rights if Selznick refused. Selznick acted, embarking on an enterprise that would consume his — and the nation's — attention for years.

Trouble began for Margaret almost with the signing of the contract.

The contract included a clause that would profit and burden her. She agreed to protect the novel's copyright from foreign infringement (her contract with Macmillan covered only American and Canadian publication), mostly to prevent a quickly made film based on a pirated edition. Because of the agreement, she spent the rest of her life at the center of a multinational vortex (and helped bring American publishers and writers under the terms of the Berne Copyright Convention, thereby assuring worldwide royalties for American authors.)

"Tighter," Scarlett pleads. Mammy (Hattie McDaniel) doesn't think it's "fittin'"—the behavior, not the corset.

The verbal agreement that she would not be involved in the film did not shelter her from hundreds of aspiring performers who sought introductions to Selznick, George Cukor (first of the film's four directors), members of Selznick's publicity department. She reported — half-incredulous, half-amused — that for months dozens of would-be Scarletts tumbled through her door, telegraphed, phoned, wrote pleading letters. They alternated with stage mothers and tapping imitation Shirley Temples in tow. Nor did it shield Margaret from repeated Hollywood inquiries — including one to evaluate Sidney Howard's 400-page screenplay.

At the height of the who-will-play-Scarlett furor, she was incorrectly quoted as supporting Katharine Hepburn for the role, a rumor based on Margaret's casual comment that she enjoyed the actress in *Little Women* and thought she looked pretty in hoop skirts. Her denial concluded: "I have never expressed a preference and never will."

Others vigorously expressed their

Scarlett sneaks away from siesta at Twelve Oaks.

preferences. Support for Gable was overwhelming, leading to contractual negotiations between Selznick and his father-in-law, Louis B. Mayer, head of Metro-Goldwyn-Mayer. The Selznick-MGM arrangement made it feasible for Selznick to finance the film and use Gable. (It helped bridge MGM's troubled waters in Hollywood's lean Fifties and Sixties.) Before he signed Gable, Selznick also considered Warner Baxter and Basil Rathbone.

Not counting the unknowns — 1,400 actresses were interviewed, 90 were tested — the contenders for Scarlett comprise a *Who's Who* of late 1930s Hollywood players. Mayer suggested, during the bargaining for Gable's services, that MGM produce the film, using studio players Maureen O'Sullivan as Melanie, Melvyn Douglas as Ashley, and Joan Crawford as Scarlett.

In retrospect, several proposed Scarletts suggest Selznick's mounting desperation and make the decision to cast an unknown appear wise. In addition to Crawford and Hepburn, contenders were Jean Arthur, Lucille Ball, Tallulah Bankhead (later offered the role of Belle Watling), Joan Bennett, Claudette Colbert, Bette Davis, Irene Dunne, Paulette Goddard, Jean Harlow, Susan Hayward, Miriam Hopkins, Carole Lombard, Norma Shearer, Ann Sheridan, Lana Turner, Loretta Young.

Self-cast contenders included an actress known as "Honey Chile" who hounded director Cukor during his Atlanta visit, and a woman who had herself delivered to Selznick's office dressed in hoop skirts and enclosed in a reproduction of the novel's cover.

Several women's groups objected to Paulette Goddard, who was nearly signed for the role, because of her relationship with Charles Chaplin, then considered scandalous. Their Mexican marriage certificate was not produced; she lost the part. The Atlanta Woman's Club urged that Miriam Hopkins be cast: A Georgia-born actress seemed to them best suited to play Scarlett. Warner Brothers Studios insisted Bette Davis be part of a package deal with Errol Flynn as Rhett, but moviegoers insisted on Gable, Selznick needed his father-in-law's financing, and Bette Davis was reluctant to appear opposite Flynn.

In return for Gable, at a higher salary than MGM was paying him (the studio kept the surplus), MGM contributed $1,250,000 — half of the film's projected production costs — and reserved world distribution rights plus half the movie's profits.

Selznick's deal with United Artists (for distribution) did not expire until the end of 1938, causing a two-year delay between securing the rights and beginning the film. The

Newly widowed Scarlett dances for charity, but the Bazaar is scandalized.

delay fed the nation's Scarlett fever, gave the producer time to promote his massively popular property, but also created difficulties and rumors that led Hollywood to refer to the movie as a white elephant, a turkey, "Selznick's folly."

Between the staging of the crumbling of Atlanta and the film's completion in July, 1939, it employed four directors (Cukor, Sam Wood, Cameron Menzies, and Victor Fleming — the last received sole credit); more than a dozen writers (including Ben Hecht, who admitted later that he never read the novel; F. Scott Fitzgerald, and Sidney Howard; only the Pulitzer Prize winning playwright received mention in the film credits); 60 leading and supporting actors; more than 2,400 extras (Selznick refused to divulge the number of manikins used in the famous crane shot of wounded and dying Confederate soldiers) and 1,000 animals. More than 400,000 feet of film were shot.

Selznick added overhead costs to the production, bringing an expenditure of $3,700,000 to a total of $4,250,000.

As of now, the film's international gross exceeds $100 million; and its one-time TV rental (for 1976 airing)

Ashley (Leslie Howard) and sister India Wilkes (Alicia Rhett—one of few screen-tested unknowns in movie)

Church becomes Confederate hospital; Scarlett and Melanie (Olivia de Havilland) tend a wounded soldier.

Scarlett makes her way through wounded soldiers to seek help in delivering Melanie's child.

Peachtree Street during evacuation of Atlanta

Scarlett, Rhett and Prissy (Butterfly McQueen) during flight from Atlanta under siege

"From the MGM release 'GONE WITH THE WIND' © 1939 Selznick International Pictures, Inc. Renewed 1967 Metro-Goldwyn-Mayer Inc."

Scarlett with grief-crazed father, Gerald O'Hara (Thomas Mitchell)

"From the MGM release 'GONE WITH THE WIND' © 1939 Selznick International Pictures, Inc. Renewed 1967 Metro-Goldwyn-Mayer Inc."

Atlanta-born Evelyn Keyes as Suellen O'Hara complaining to Mammy

Scarlett encounters marauding Union soldier at war-ravaged Tara.

Scarlett with "Pork" (Oscar Polk)

adds $5 million. To produce the film today would cost an estimated $35 million.

On December 15, 1939, the world premiere of *Gone With the Wind* was celebrated in Atlanta — and festivities lasted for days. Some 300,000 persons attended a Five Points-to-Georgian Terrace Hotel parade which featured 50 bands. Celebrities poured in; Gov. E. D. Rivers declared a state holiday; Mayor William B. Hartsfield proclaimed a three-day festival, urging Atlantans to grow beards and sideburns and wear 19th Century costumes.

The facade of Loew's Grand Theater was decorated to resemble the film version of Tara. Sketches of the Hollywood set amused Margaret because of its pretentious overdressing of the casual back-country house she had imagined: "We were laughing on the floor."

The theater seated just over 2,000

Study in contrasts: Melanie converses with Belle Watling (Ona Munson).

Rhett admires Scarlett in her honeymoon finery.

BEHIND THE SCENES....

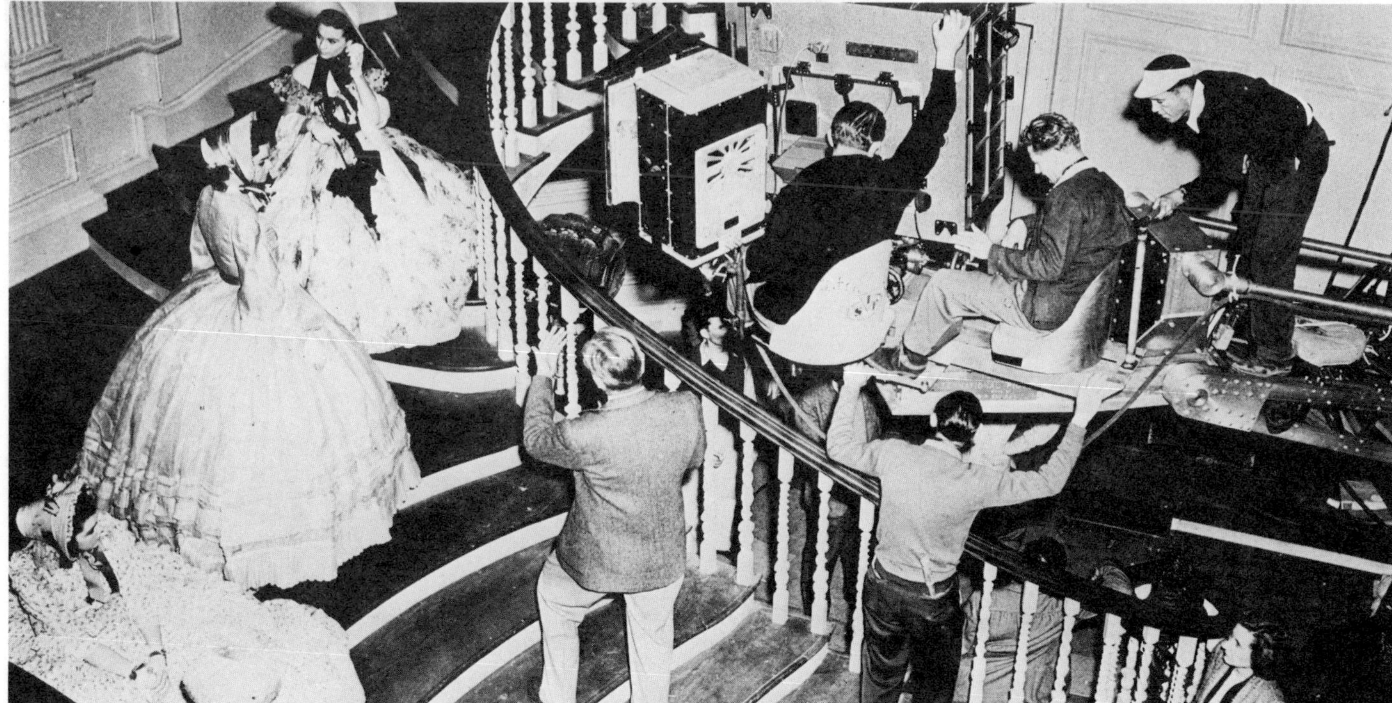

Film's painstaking attention to detail is typified by Twelve Oaks' elaborate staircase.

"From the MGM release 'GONE WITH THE WIND' © 1939 Selznick International Pictures, Inc. Renewed 1967 Metro-Goldwyn-Mayer Inc."

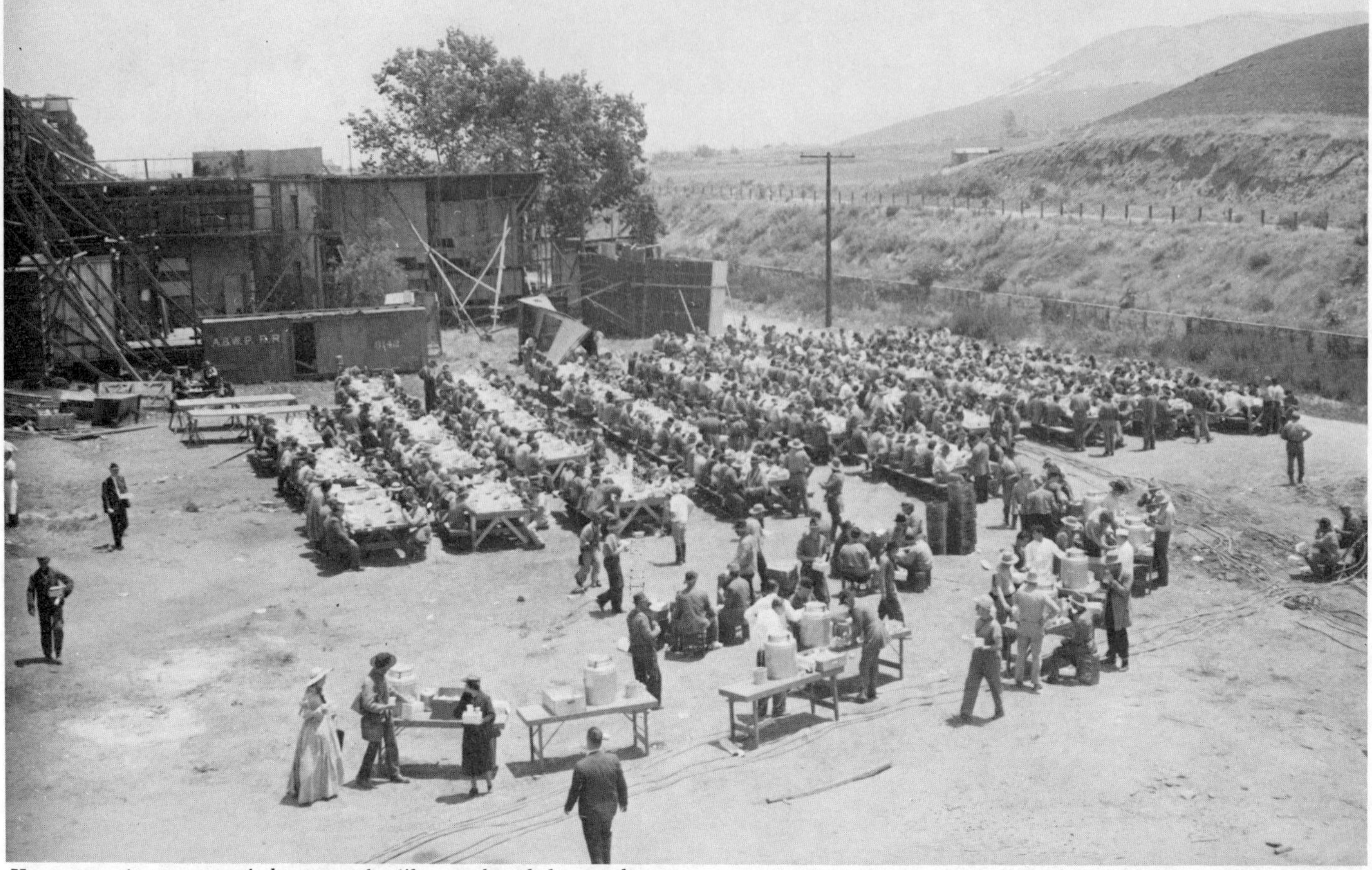

Huge cast of extras was fed army style; film employed thousands.

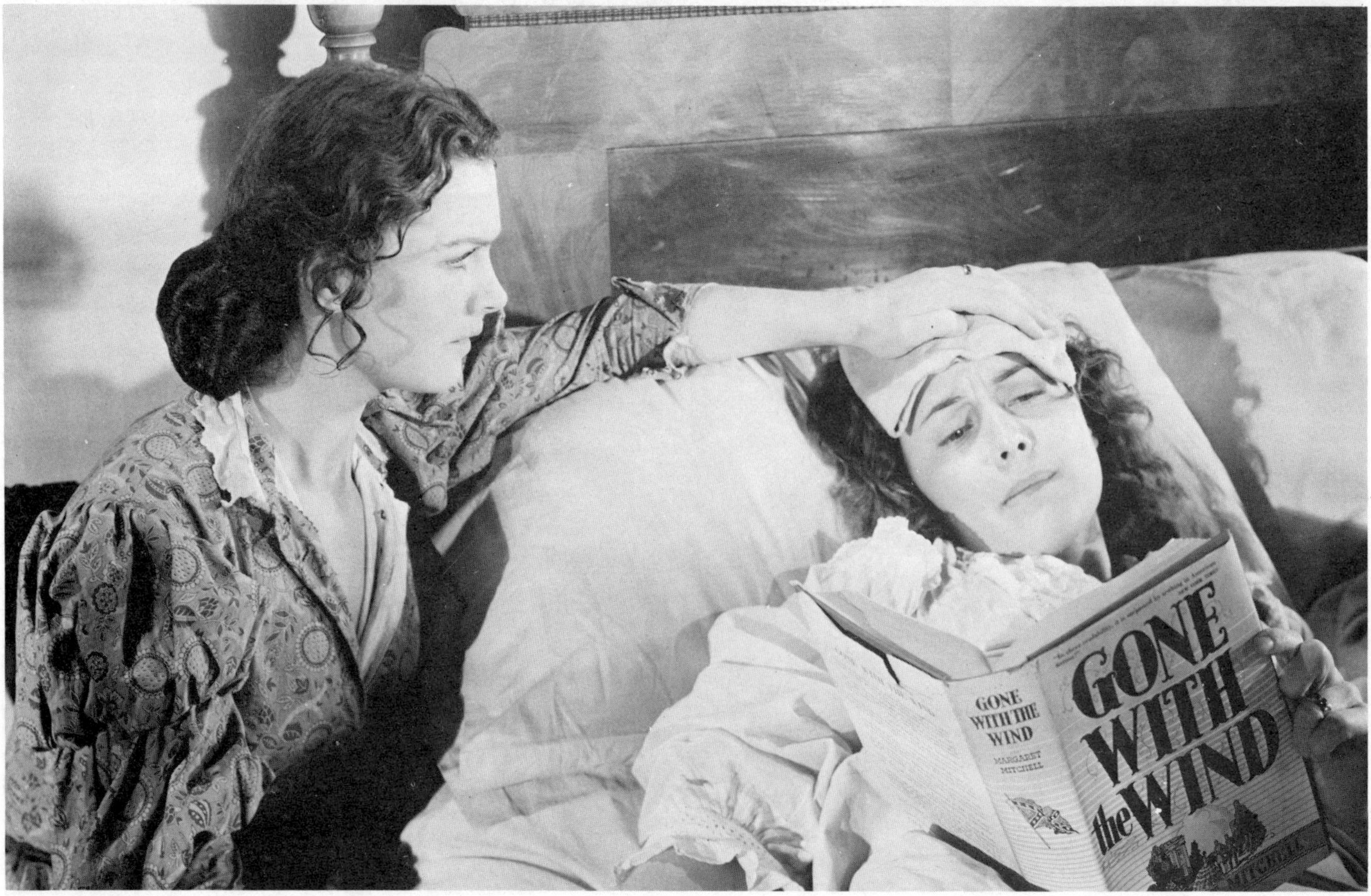

Off-camera break. Vivien Leigh coveted role, but later admitted: "I didn't like Scarlett."

TARA: REEL AND REAL

The painting (at left) by Atlanta's famed Wilbur G. Kurtz served as the model for "Gone With the Wind's" film version of Tara.

In 1959—almost exactly 20 years after "Gone With the Wind" had its world premiere in Atlanta—Norman Shavin (then TV Editor of The Atlanta Journal) visited the lot on which rested the rotting remains of moviedom's Tara (below) and its attached facades.

With Shavin (at left in each photo below, taken in 1959) is Carroll Nye, then a publicist, who portrayed Frank Kennedy, Scarlett's second husband in the film.

Courtesy Collection of Norman Shavin

Courtesy Collection of Norman Shavin

Courtesy Collection of Norman Shavin

Carroll Nye stands in the Tara doorway of "Gone With the Wind's" film version; the photo was made in 1959. Recently, all the Tara structures were taken down and sold, reportedly to be reconstructed as the world's most famous mansion.

Courtesy Collection of Norman Shavin

Courtesy Collection of Norman Shavin

Courtesy Collection of Norman Shavin

These photographs (made in 1959) were accurate Hollywood representations of Atlanta streets (above, left and right) in the Civil War era, as well as the train station (left), modeled after the one which once stood near the entrance of present-day Underground Atlanta.

filmgoers, each paying $10. (Scalpers were asking as much as $200 by opening night.) Governors of five Southern states attended, along with some Whitneys and Rockefellers, the David Selznicks, his brother Myron, and a galaxy of actors and actresses. From the cast came Leigh, Gable, Olivia de Havilland, Ann Rutherford, Laura Hope Crews, Evelyn Keyes, Thomas Mitchell, Ona Munson, and a few non-*GWTW* celebrities — Claudette Colbert, Carole Lombard (Mrs. Clark Gable), and Laurence Olivier (Vivien Leigh's fiancé).

And Margaret. At the end of the film, she said the actors had spoken more eloquently than she could and praised the "absolutely perfect cast."

A charity ball preceded the premiere in Municipal Auditorium, its stage decorated with Tara's columns and the auditorium decked to resemble the film's Charity Bazaar. The ball was sponsored by the Junior League — the organization that had refused to admit Margaret to membership almost 20 years before.

Gone With the Wind opened nationally with rave reviews. *Variety's* notice called it "a great picture" and predicted "grosses which may be second to none in the history of the business."

Frank Nugent's *New York Times* film review was succinct and accurate: "It is pure narrative, as the novel was, rather than great drama, as the novel was not . . . you will leave it, not with the feeling you have undergone a profound emotional experience, but with the warm and grateful remembrance of an interesting story beautifully told. Is it the greatest motion picture ever made? Probably not, although it is the greatest motion mural we have seen and the most ambitious film-making venture in Hollywood's spectacular history."

Gone With the Wind added to that spectacular history. By the end of its first run six months later, more than 25 million had seen it.

It was included in *The New York Times*' "Top Ten Films" of the year, and in February, 1940, received a then record-breaking 10 Academy Awards: best picture; best actress (Leigh); best supporting actress

Courtesy Atlanta Journal-Constitution Sunday Magazine

Legends meet: Clark Gable and Margaret Mitchell.

Courtesy of Lane Brothers Photography

Premiere attracted all-star cast: (front row, left to right) Herbert Bayard Swope, Claudette Colbert, Irene (Mrs. David) Selznick, Georgia Governor E. D. Rivers; (second row) John Hay Whitney, Margaret Mitchell, John Marsh, Clark Cable, Carole Lombard (Mrs. Gable), Atlanta Mayor William B. Hartsfield.

(Hattie McDaniel; the first black actress to receive an Oscar, she was also awarded a special citation by the NAACP); best director (Fleming); best screenplay (Howard, who had been killed in an accident the year before; his award was accepted by Sinclair Lewis); best photography (Ernest Haller and Ray Rennahan); design and color (Cameron Menzies); best art direction (Lyle Wheeler); best editing (Hal Kern and James Newcom); special effects (Jack Cosgrove). The Irving Thalberg Memorial Award for production achievement was given Selznick.

Thomas Mitchell, the film's Gerald O'Hara, received the Academy Award for best supporting actor for his performance in *Stagecoach* the same year. Gable lost to Robert Donat (for *Goodbye, Mr. Chips),* but had received an Oscar for his performance in *It Happened One Night* (1934). Olivia de Havilland, the film's Melanie, received Oscars later as best actress in *To Each His Own* (1946) and *The Heiress* (1949). Leigh was awarded a second Oscar for *A Streetcar Named Desire* (1951).

Gone With the Wind was shown in London for three years during the "blitz" of World War II. It played for four years without interruption in Paris following the city's liberation in 1944, and was playing in Jerusalem in February, 1974, during Mideast fighting.

Margaret would also do her share during World War II.

CHAPTER VI

THE RELUCTANT CELEBRITY

"Did Scarlett get Rhett back?"

The question haunted readers of *Gone With the Wind* for years. They hounded Margaret to learn what happened to Scarlett after the end of the novel. Her answer never varied: She had no idea what happened to her characters. She finished her story in 1,037 pages; for her, that ended it.

What happened to Margaret in the 10 years between the film's release and her accidental death *is* known.

Among other pressures, she coped with thousands of requests for material, whether or not related to *Gone With the Wind*. Requests came even from Selznick, anxious to duplicate the film's success. In February, 1940, he sent a memo to Kay Brown referring to a possible sequel. Margaret refused.

In October, 1941, he proposed a film, *The Daughter of Scarlett O'-Hara,* starring Vivien Leigh. He informed Kay Brown he "was willing to pay plenty" for a novel, a novelette, "even a short story." Admitting that "we killed off Bonnie Blue," he suggested — Scarlett being Scarlett— it would be easy to arrange a fourth husband and a pregnancy. Margaret refused.

Why was there no other fiction by Margaret after *Gone With the Wind?*

It was reported Margaret contemplated writing a play about the impact of fame on a couple like the John Marshes, but any works-in-progress will never be known. In observance of her instructions, John Marsh and Margaret Baugh — the secretary hired after the publication of *Gone With the Wind* — destroyed all surviving manuscripts after her death. Among known works were fragments of an abandoned Jazz Age novel, detailing the lifestyle of the Twenties through its heroine, Pansy Hamilton. Her completed work included a novella, *'Ropa Carmigan,* named for a heroine — Europa — whose character can only be imagined. Lois Cole said the novella was chillingly effective, and The Macmillan Company thought it publishable — its brevity was a problem, however, and it was never offered by Margaret to another publisher.

Margaret admires medals of one of last surviving Confederate veterans.

Courtesy Atlanta Journal-Constitution Sunday Magazine

Her letters give clues as to why she wrote nothing else, and amplify her personality.

She wrote long, carefully worded, thorough letters: answers to friends, authors (Benét, John P. Marquand, Marjorie Rawlings, others), strangers whose letters intrigued her, agents, publishers, lawyers, columnists and writers who described a Margaret different from the real person and whose likeness she did not want to be spread.

Stephens recalls one of her characteristic expressions: "When a fact and a theory collide, the fact always loses — except for very smart people." Determined that what was said of her be fact, her whittling of the many Margaret Mitchell legends was time consuming.

In August, 1944, she was still readable copy for Hollywood's most widely read gossiper, Louella Parsons. Referring to Margaret as the author of *Gone With the Wind* who "then did nothing else, not even a short story," she reported: "It's about time she wrote another story, and one of our top producers sent her a blank check bearing his signature, with the request she write an original for the screen. P.S. The check came back."

Eight years earlier Margaret had asked Parsons to quash the rumor that she was going blind. In 1944 Margaret again wrote the columnist: "I could not have sent back the check, because the check was non-existent. There has been no time for me to do any writing of any nature since *Gone With the Wind* was published."

Her letter concludes: "I would appreciate very much if you would put the true facts about this in your column. I am trying to get back to my work at the Red Cross but am so hampered by inquiries resulting from false rumors that I am prevented from doing the work I would like to do."

The reply is an illuminating glimpse of the fame-weary author trying to live a quiet life, refusing to occupy a house of rumor, gossip and legend as false as Hollywood's Tara.

She was now deeply involved in the war effort: as air raid warden, seller of Savings Stamps and War Bonds, Red Cross volunteer who wrapped bandages and rang doorbells to enlist blood donors, and busy writer of letters to servicemen. Bill Mauldin paid her tribute in a "GI Joe" cartoon depicting a frazzled soldier writing to "Dear Miss Mitchell." She had christened the cruiser "Atlanta" in 1941. After it was sunk in battle, she christened a new "Atlanta" whose cost had been paid through War Bonds sold by Margaret.

She attended her father throughout his illness, just as she nursed John after her husband's heart attack in 1945. Despite her repeated insistence that she was not the author of autobiographical characters, almost 25 years after Margaret's death it would be said of her that in her last years she became Melanie-like.

Margaret was neither Scarlett nor Melanie nor a fiction in between. She was a fiercely independent and private person. The welfare of her immediate family was a powerful bond, a concern that also embraced friends, servants, even strangers who had been treated unjustly. Yet, her compassion was seasoned with the salt of independence: She bore long grudges, nursed old enmities, and chose to love individuals rather than humankind, an abstraction. Stephens summarizes the values she prized: "She stood . . . for order, for freedom, against prejudice and injustice."

The letter to Louella Parsons proves she was not a shy little person who stumbled from a provincial island into global fame. She stood tall for her rights from the time of her novel's initial success to her death: the right to privacy, to protect the product of her imagination, to accuracy in public references to her.

It was impossible for Margaret to maintain complete privacy. She was a public figure, self-described as an

Courtesy U.S. Navy

Margaret christens cruiser Atlanta, September, 1941, in Kearny, N. J.

Courtesy Atlanta Journal-Constitution Sunday Magazine

Margaret, assisted by Bessie Jordan, prepares relief parcels for post-war Europe (1947). The cat? Maud.

"unpaid greeter for the Chamber of Commerce." Though she refused to be treated as an impersonal monument, as public property, she willingly performed public services she deemed worthy. Charities received her time and money.

The Florence Crittenton Home for unwed mothers was especially important to her. She worked with prisoners in the Atlanta Federal Penitentiary, offering prizes to the work of the best writers there. She attended luncheons honoring writers living in or visiting Atlanta. She was cordial to celebrities she met, but respected their privacy as much as she treasured hers.

Partly because of the contractual agreement with Selznick which made copyright protection her responsibility, but also because she was descended from a family who prized law and ethical behavior, she became immersed in international copyright law.

The most far-reaching legal test was heard before the Netherlands Supreme Court in an action brought by Margaret against Zuid-Hollandsche Uitgeuers Maatschappij (ZHUM). Canada was a participant in the Berne Convention, and The Macmillan Company had published a Canadian edition simultaneously with the American printing. ZHUM claimed the Canadian issue was only a token printing. The Dutch Supreme Court decided in Margaret's favor on May 10, 1941 (the day Germany invaded the Lowlands). Since World War II ended, ZHUM annually sends tulips to be planted at her grave.

With the German takeover of publishers in subjugated countries, she was affected by the War before the United States entered it. She knew of Nazi and Communist suppression of her novel and the film in occupied countries, and that escalated her already fierce distaste for totalitarian government.

Margaret was as independent politically as she was personally. She had defied Prohibition on principle, as a moral duty against a ridiculous, unenforceable law. Asked at a Capital City Club meeting by an *Atlanta Journal* representative to write a weekly column, she responded heatedly that she was "a story teller and not a columnist, an editorialist or a person who could write critical and evaluation stuff." She identified herself as an "anti-New Deal and old fashioned Democrat . . . I said I believed in the old fashioned idea that it was the duty of every patriotic American citizen to resist the Government in every way possible, beginning with keep-off-the-grass signs and working up through income taxes . . ." She paid her taxes ungrudgingly, however, and felt that taxes should have been even higher to pay the costs of World War II without burdening future generations with debt.

Her memo summarizing the meeting ends with a swift display of temper and humor: "I am sure everyone in the Capital City Club heard the conversation because I was so deaf from my cold that [my companion] had to yell to make himself understood. I was yelling too, and several visiting firemen at the next table turned to stare frankly when I said that I thought the duty of a citizen involved, too, the calling of sons of bitches 'sons of bitches' every time they acted like sons of bitches."

No, she was not Melanie.

Nor, despite such flashes of temper, was she Scarlett.

She was Margaret Mitchell. She met the shocks of life with equanimity, remembering what she already knew: The heights are as harrowing as the hollows, and fortune is capricious as the wind.

In her life she endured much pain; hours before *Gone With the Wind's* premiere she wrenched her back and was uncomfortably bandaged; she suffered loss, grief, early sorrow.

Margaret and John struggled through the Depression to pay his medical debts, uncomplainingly accepting the challenge as a jagged discord of the joyous Jazz Age.

Her life contained the wheat of legend; it is easy to cast her as the little woman who wrote the big book. Closer to truth is the hard working researcher who assured the vitality of her book through detail mined from months of dusty fact-hunting. *Gone With the Wind* is vivid because it is fiction spun from fact.

Gone With the Wind is not propagandistic, not political, not polemical. It has been faulted because it does not explore the plight of antebellum blacks or trace the causes of the Civil War, but that, as Margaret answered some of her critics, is not the novel she intended or wrote.

The book needs no apology, for either its content or its craft. If it is not "The Great American Novel," as its paperback edition claims, it is statistically the most popular American novel.

Beneath its escapism and beyond its love story is a compelling saga of survival in a world turned upside down. Rereading the novel in the Seventies, it is as if Margaret Mitchell led readers down the road to Jonesboro, warning — as she was warned by her mother — "when your world explodes, God help you if you don't have some weapon to meet the new

Courtesy Atlanta Journal-Constitution Sunday Magazine

In a City Hall celebration marking Atlanta's 100th year (1948), Margaret sliced a birthday cake, handing a piece to Mayor William B. Hartsfield.

world." And as Stephens comments, Mammy stands at our shoulder, cautioning us of behavior which is fitting and that which is not.

Perhaps the novel's continuing hold on the imagination was summarized best by Olivia de Havilland, the film's Melanie. After the movie's re-premiere in Atlanta in 1967, she wrote in *Look* magazine: "I looked at Scarlett, and knew she meant survival, the physical survival of a vanquished people; and I looked at Melanie, and I knew she meant survival, too, the spiritual survival of the values and traditions of a lost civilization, and I understood why, for countries all over the world who have known conflict and defeat and survival, *Gone With the Wind* is their story."

* * *

On the night of August 11, 1949, crossing Peachtree Street with her husband John to see a British movie, *A Canterbury Tale,* Margaret Mitchell Marsh was struck by a speeding car. She lay hospitalized in a coma five days.

She died August 16, fewer than 10 years after the movie was premiered in Atlanta. During the five days of her dying, Atlanta newspapers and Grady Memorial Hospital were deluged by grieving inquiries.

In his unpublished memoir, Stephens writes: "The long train of automobiles went to Oakland Cemetery. It is the old city cemetery, set up in 1850. Across the valley loom the great buildings of the new city and the sun bounces back from the ranks of their windows to the country town graveyard near their midst. They buried her there beside her father and her mother and her little brother who died in babyhood. There was a grave space left for John. The flowers were banked high. I forgot to tell the caretakers to give the flowers to the crowd. I did it the next day. There was a crowd there for two or three days. She had said something to her people and they had answered."

Now (25 years after her death), when asked what she had said to her people Stephens replied by quoting the Mitchell family motto, from *Ecclesiastes:*

"The race is not to the swift, nor the battle to the strong, neither yet bread to the wise, nor yet riches to men of understanding, nor yet favour to men of skill; but time and chance happeneth to them all."

From the Estate of Margaret Mitchell; courtesy Stephens Mitchell

Margaret's last picture, made in the summer of 1949 (weeks before she died). It was taken by Cone Maddox, a friend of the Mitchell family. She would have been 49 on November 8, 1949.

CHAPTER VII

TRACES OF THE LEGEND

The "tomorrow" that Scarlett O'Hara spoke of applies poetically to the life of Margaret Mitchell's book, as the following pictures illustrate. "Gone With the Wind" lives, in its film version, and transmutations to stage; Margaret herself is remembered by other traces of tribute in Atlanta.

Courtesy Atlanta Journal-Constitution Sunday Magazine

Mr. and Mrs. Stephens Mitchell chat with Vivien Leigh, Douglas Fairbanks Jr., George Murphy, David O. Selznick and Olivia de Havilland during film's Atlanta re-showing of film (1961) to mark 100th anniversary of the start of the Civil War.

Courtesy Atlanta Journal-Constitution Sunday Magazine

Decades after its first release, GWTW still drew crowds—and still does.

Bronze plaque marks Margaret's childhood home.

From the Estate of Margaret Mitchell; courtesy Stephens Mitchell

Atlanta street sign

Courtesy Collection of Norman Shavin

Margaret Mitchell School, on Atlanta's Margaret Mitchell Drive, is in the fashionable northwest section.

Courtesy Collection of Norman Shavin

Atlanta Public Library's main branch pays tribute, too.

Courtesy Atlanta Public Library

Courtesy Atlanta Chamber of Commerce

ATLANTA . . .

ATLANTA'S DOWNTOWN TODAY. ITS

Courtesy Collection of Norman Shavin

This was wartime Atlanta, 1864, before federal troops burned the city. In the foreground is Whitehall Street where army wagons waited to cross the tracks. The passenger depot, adjacent to present-day Underground Atlanta, is at left. The "Rock Depot" of the Macon & Western Railroad is in the middle center.

Courtesy Atlanta Chamber of Commerce

NOW AND THEN

GROWTH MIGHT HAVE STARTLED HER.

Courtesy Collection of Norman Shavin

This extraordinary skyview of downtown Atlanta is an 1889 photograph, and shows the remarkable comeback Atlanta was making 25 years after Sherman burned it (see next page). The photo was made 11 years before Margaret Mitchell was born, representing the city much as she knew it as a child.

Courtesy Collection of Norman Shavin

Desolation marks the site (left) where several ammunition trains were exploded by retreating Confederates as Sherman moved to possess Atlanta.

In 1876 (photo below) Atlanta was struggling to rebuild, the picture of the intersection of Pryor and Alabama Streets suggesting scenes Scarlett O'Hara knew in days of Reconstruction. The pictured area is now the site of Underground Atlanta.

Courtesy Collection of Norman Shavin

Courtesy Collection of Norman Shavin

"Gone With the Wind's" themes of survival and courage have for decades entranced peoples oppressed. These photos, made in 1974, are outside a theater where the film was being offered—in Hebrew—in Jerusalem.

Courtesy Collection of Norman Shavin

CHAPTER VIII

SCARLETT ON STAGE

Scarlett's career on stage has been colorful and complicated.

Margaret Mitchell's contract with Selznick reserved all stage rights to the author, and there were several occasions which prompted her to protect those rights.

Without securing the author's permission, showman Billy Rose included a musical version of *Gone With the Wind* in his Fort Worth Frontier Fiesta production. *Variety's* review commented: "Harriet Hoctor is the Scarlett O'Hara of his version of Margaret Mitchell's weighty volume, and in a few minutes on her toes she wipes out a good 600 pages of the original work. The setting for Tara, schemed by Albert Johnson, is one of the most spacious edifices ever to crowd a stage. Its facade must stretch across a good 200 feet, and it towers up a full three stories. Three hundred singers, dancers and pantomimists participate in this Dixie lament which ends with Union troopers burning the O'Hara mansion to the ground."

When the suit was entered against him, Rose invited the Marshes to attend the production, certain that the author would approve of his version. John Marsh refused, and Margaret Mitchell wrote that the showman responded: "It's pretty well known that Mrs. Marsh is averse to . . . publicity. Well, I'll fix her. I'll make her come to Fort Worth to testify and she will get more publicity than she wants." John Marsh replied calmly: "Mrs. Marsh thought over that possibility before entering suit and is prepared to do what she must do."

Billy Rose paid the author $3,000 in damages, pledged an additional $25,000 if he violated her rights again, and sent her a letter of apology.

In November, 1966, a properly licensed stage version of *Gone With the Wind* opened in Japan. Based on the first half of the novel, the production lasted five hours. After a five-month run, it was followed by Part Two, which required four hours. Part Two had a four-month run. Total cost of the production equaled $1 million.

London's Drury Lane Theater, where a stage musical version of "GWTW" opened in May, 1972

Courtesy Collection of Norman Shavin

In 1970, a musical version of the dramatization, titled *Scarlett,* enjoyed an equally successful Japanese engagement.

Two years later, with music by Harold Rome and book by Horton Foote, the musical *Gone With the Wind* opened in London. It cost $500,000 to mount, and though it opened to mixed reviews, it was a popular success.

Rex Reed pronounced the London musical a bomb: "I can remember nothing in my theatre-going history I consider a bigger disaster." He singled out as the biggest show-stopping moment on opening night the behavior of Scarlett's horse as the heroine struggles to get back to Tara. "They're talking about bringing *Gone With the Wind* to Broadway," he concluded. "They must be kidding. Even if they rewrite it, recast it, restage it, rescore it, and stop feeding the horse before he goes on stage, they'll still be bringing in a wake."

Bruce Galphin's *Atlanta* Magazine review was more calm and less caustic: Director-choreographer Joe Layton's *Gone With the Wind*—"and it is his more than anyone else's—is a strong, exciting statement on its own merits, without reference to its antecedents. It is a portrait of a Southern woman whom the defeats of war and of the heart transform from a self-centered girl into a calculating woman who poisons the love of friend and family. The story is told in a series of fast-flowing tableaux which evoke mood and emotion visually as well as verbally. It is good theater."

Stephens Mitchell agrees with Galphin's estimate.

The musical was premiered in America in Los Angeles, then played in San Francisco, despite efforts to stage the American opening in Atlanta. It closed after a brief run.

Margaret Mitchell's estate still owns the stage rights to her novel, and has made contractual arrangements only with the Japanese producer. The San Francisco production was a sub-licensee of the British production, which was in turn sub-licensed from the Japanese.

What's next for *Gone With the Wind?* Telecasts of the original movie, possibly a movie sequel and also a book related to the sequel.

If it could be divorced from the by now indelible memories of book and film and condensed into an abbreviated libretto, *Gone With the Wind* has elements that call for operatic rather than stage musical treatment.

Who could write it, sing it, direct it, produce it?

Those are questions for tomorrow.

And, as Scarlett says: "Tomorrow is another day."

Courtesy Collection of Norman Shavin

Courtesy Collection of Norman Shavin

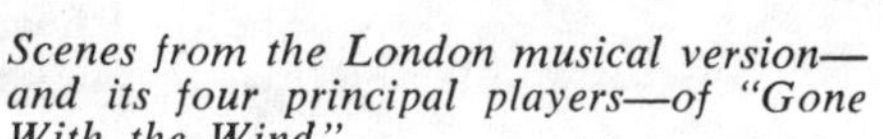

Scenes from the London musical version—and its four principal players—of "Gone With the Wind"

Courtesy Collection of Norman Shavin

CHAPTER IX

THE MORTAL AND THE IMMORTAL

For some of those associated with the filming of *Gone With the Wind,* the movie—premiered in 1939 (40 years ago)—would mark the high point of their careers.

Some would make other films of note, but all would seem immortalized by their association with the movie version of Margaret's book.

She died fewer than 10 years after its premiere; her husband died three years after she (in 1952).

And Fate played the final hand for some of the major figures associated with the film.

Leslie Howard died at 53 in 1943, killed when German planes shot down an airliner in which he was traveling from Lisbon to London.

Louis B. Mayer died in 1956.

Clark Gable was 59 when he died suddenly of a heart attack in 1960. (His wife, Carole Lombard, was 36 when she died in a plane crash in 1942.)

In 1965, David Selznick, then 63, died—and actress Katharine Hepburn recited Rudyard Kipling's "If . . ." at his funeral. Why "If"? Possibly because it had been reported that Selznick had wanted to mount a musical stage version of *Gone With the Wind*. (One was premiered—in Tokyo—the year after Selznick died.)

Vivien Leigh was suffering tuberculosis in the Fifties, causing her to drop from the role she had begun in 1954 in the movie *Elephant Walk*. (Elizabeth Taylor replaced her.) Vivien Leigh's marriage to actor Sir Laurence Olivier ended years later. Miss Leigh made other films, and appeared on stage in *Lady Of the Camellias* (the story on which Giuseppe Verdi based his brilliant opera, *La Traviata* — "the lost one", The heroine of *Traviata* dies of consumption and—if you will—a broken heart. At age 54, Vivien Leigh died — of tuberculosis — in 1967.

But alive in 1985 were Olivia de Havilland (Melanie), Butterfly McQueen (Prissy), and others.

All humans face death, but often the parts they play transcend the dying, and great themes survive. Like survival—in the face of every angry charge.

When Stephens Mitchell was making the funeral-service arrangements for Margaret, he recalls, he asked that Dean Raimundo de Ovies, of Atlanta's Protestant Episcopal Cathedral, read "The Service for the Dead from the Book of Common Prayer." And Dean de Ovies observed, "What gentlefolk would like."

The world wept with Margaret's burial in Atlanta's Oakland Cemetery, dating from 1850.

That was many yesterdays ago.

Now, there is always "tomorrow."

Always.